J T TALBOT

The Little Book Of Grieving

Introduction

Why did I become a bereavement volunteer?

Why did I write this book?

Some years ago, I was working in the NHS in a department dealing with end of life care packages for terminally ill patients, supporting the administration of this process. Although I wasn't involved clinically I was still very involved in ensuring patients received the best possible service 'to live as well as possible and to die with dignity' (reference https://www.nhs.uk/conditions/end-of-life-care/what-it-involves-and-when-it-starts/). At times, it could be stressful so I enrolled myself on a two-day Mental Health First Aider course. It was whilst on this course, I learned of an opportunity to train as a bereavement volunteer. I enrolled and that is where my journey in grief work began.

Rather naively, I thought I had a good understanding of grieving. Like many people, I have experienced numerous family and friends dying over the years. But this volunteer training taught me so much more about the multi-faceted and overwhelming effect of grief – on your emotions, on the body/mind connection, and on relationships within families, social groups and in the workplace. I distinctly remember thinking 'how can I not know all this stuff about death and grief? Everyone should have a crash course in how to deal with grief'. It is that belief that we can all benefit from talking more openly and sharing our experiences of grief and grieving that has led me to write this book.

Together with my bereavement training, my health and social care degree has allowed me to deepen my knowledge and enhance my practice with clients who have lost a loved one. I understand only too well how grief impacts upon mental health, how unresolved and complicated grief can lead to more complex anxiety, depression, substance abuse, eating disorders, crime and, even, suicide.

I say in my book that at some time in our lives we will all be affected by death and loss. This is certainly true for me. Whilst writing this book, I have experienced the deaths of two very dear and much-loved family members. It caused me to pause the writing of this book at times, but it has also enriched these pages with first-hand experiences drawn from my own grieving. Sadly, I was not alone in my grief as some of my friends and work colleagues suffered bereavements too. I have been able to capture elements of all these personal grief stories and weave them anonymously into this book. Everyone grieves – and as a Bereavement Volunteer I also rest and take a break from supporting clients when I am grieving. I have to be well and in a good mental space to help others. It is our intrinsic human nature to grieve, just as it is the nature of flowers to bloom and stars to sparkle and shine.

I want this book to reach out to you if you want to know more about:

- What grieving looks and feels like in your mind and body
- How to cope with loss
- How you can help others – family, friends, colleagues - who are grieving

Saying a final goodbye to someone you love is one of the most emotional experiences you will endure. Grief caused by death, loss and change can have a powerful effect on your life. Given that grief will visit us all at one time or another, this book will – I hope – help some of you find your personal pathway to understanding and managing your grief.

I have kept the format simple so the book is easy to read. There is a 'Notes' section at the back of the book so you can jot things down as you go along and refer back to them. This may be helpful if your memory and concentration are being affected by grieving as I know mine were.

If, from this book, you learn that grieving is a natural reaction to death and loss, that grieving can look and feel differently for all, that you can learn how to grieve, cope and support one another, then I will have achieved what I set out to do. I really do hope you find this book useful to you in your time of sadness and need.

Contents

Introduction   i

Chapter 1 - Shying away from the D words   1

Chapter 2 - Genuine Reactions to Grief   9

Chapter 3 - Change, Loss and Grieving   22

Chapter 4 - Your Goodbyes   27

Chapter 5 - How to Cope   34

Chapter 6 - Different Ways of Remembering   47

Chapter 7 - Living with Grief   57

Chapter 8 - Supporting those who are Grieving   64

Chapter 9 - Support   72

A Final Word   76

References   78

Chapter 1 -
Shying away from the D words

What led you to a book about grieving?

Is it because you know someone who has been bereaved and you want to understand more about grief to help them?

Or does it feel like a piece of you is missing and you need to know why you feel so broken-hearted?

If, like many of my clients, you still can't believe it's real, that it actually happened and you're struggling to cope, that your life is spiralling out of control and you feel like you're going 'a bit mad' then I understand. You've done the right thing. You have come to the right place. This book can help you.

The effects of grief can be agonising, gut-wrenching, heart-breaking, soul destroying and extremely tiring. Pouring over every little detail of the how, when, where, who, what and why. Spending hours processing these thoughts as well as the layers of information drawn from snippets of conversation from those involved alongside your own thoughts. It is exhausting and you just want it all to go away. But you need to know it won't always be this way. You won't always feel this way.

Everything you are feeling is a genuine reaction to grief. You may be finding it difficult to talk right now or express how you feel, but all this is to be expected. Death and grieving are so difficult to discuss even with our nearest and dearest. It can feel really uncomfortable starting a conversation about death and if you do, it's not that easy is it?

Let's face it, talking about the death of a loved one can seem impossibly painful, both for the person speaking the words and for the listener hearing them. Lots of awkward silences, 'let's just change the subject' moments or 'let's ignore it completely' chats. I wonder if it has always been this way or if it is the same across the world and with all cultures?

In years gone by, mourning - a public display of wailing and crying - was expected. It was a part of the 'death package', with some cultures even having professional mourners in attendance at death ceremonies.

Whilst times have changed and our modern world has progressed in many ways, it feels like we have regressed in terms of using the words; *'death'*, *'dying'*, *'died'*, *'dead'* and *'deceased'*. These words are taboo in contemporary conversation and even typing, writing and texting them can feel awkward.

Avoiding using the D words somehow feels ignorant, like death is being denied and therefore the period which naturally follows death, which we know as grieving, feels forbidden, unmentionable and off-limits. Not using the correct terminology is like saying grieving is not allowed. Unsurprisingly, this does not make it all go away. Stifling how we feel is so unnatural, especially at a time when we actually need more compassion, understanding and love. We need to be turning towards grieving, not turning away from it. Grief serves a purpose. It is there for a reason and should never be suppressed, ignored or denied.

Take Julie, after the death of her father she received the following text messages from friends:

'I am so sorry for your loss'

'Thinking of you and sending my condolences'

I wonder why they didn't feel they could text the following instead:

'I'm so sorry to hear your dad has died'

'Thinking of you after the death of your father and sending my condolences'

Are we afraid that these words feel too harsh and too final when related to the death of a person because death is the end of living (1)?

When we refer to other things - plants, flowers, animals and even batteries, we use the D words quite naturally. We say 'the flowers have died' not 'the flowers have passed away'. The flowers have not 'gone, 'left' nor have you 'lost' them; yet all these common expressions are used instead of the D words when talking about a human subject.

From an early age we learn about nature, the life cycle and we know that death is a part of this picture. But why is it so difficult to talk about when people are involved? Why are we scared to use the correct words at appropriate times - is it that:

- Talking about it makes it real
- You don't know what to say/you've never been taught what to say
- You're not sure how best to phrase your words
- You fear you may say the wrong thing
- You think you may make the person feel worse not better
- You worry about how they will react to what you say or do
- You believe you'll make them cry
- You just don't know what to say for the best, so it's better not to say anything

If you've been bereaved, then it's common to feel as though the death is being ignored or avoided in conversations.It can feel as if those around you 'are treading on egg shells' or 'skirting round the issue' instead of actually acknowledging what has happened and how you may be feeling.

You may not be the 'normal' you after a bereavement but isn't this to be expected? Shouldn't your circle of friends/family/ colleagues know, acknowledge and make allowances for you not being your 'usual self'?

Shouldn't a bereavement be a time for extra support, understanding and knowing? *Shouldn't we all know how to console someone?*

After the death of Jeremy's step-mum some of his friends never said 'I'm sorry to hear about your step-mum' and simply engaged in normal conversation. There was no acknowledgment of her death. This really hurt Jeremy's feelings and he felt it was deeply disrespectful.

Don't worry if you don't, you're not alone. Knowing how to comfort and support the bereaved can be so hard to deal with and it often feels much easier to avoid it altogether.

- You don't' know what to say (they don't know what they want you to say)
- You don't know what to do (they don't know what they want you to do)

Your closest friends and family may avoid talking about your miscarriage, your mum dying from cancer, your partner's suicide, your colleague's unexpected heart attack, your dog dying from old age.

The adverse consequences of this reluctance to discuss death can have a knock-on effect upon the natural grieving process. After the funeral is over, a grieving person knows that they are expected to carry on as normal, keep their thoughts/feelings private, hide their emotions and resume their life, work etc. by not talking about 'it' and carrying on as if nothing has happened.

Also, in our fast paced world, it can feel as if:

- You don't have time to spend grieving, life is too busy
- It is an additional thing 'to do', it's inconvenient or unnecessary
- It will be too emotional, too painful, too hurtful and you just 'can't go there'

If you can relate to the above, you are not alone.

In fact, every minute of every day someone, somewhere in the world dies.

In the UK, there are around 600,000 deaths per year (2)

This means lots of people grieving, right now.

Rather more, it also means there are immediate and extended family, friends, colleagues, neighbours of the bereaved all not knowing how to best support those grieving. Others do too. Talking openly and factually about death and grief as a natural part of life matters to all of us and is especially beneficial to your health and wellbeing. This is echoed by the Public Health England/NHS campaign, 'Every Mind Matters' (3) who offer 'expert advice and practical tips to look after your mental health and wellbeing and information on how to deal with grief and loss'.

> Death and dying are a natural part of life. Grieving is to be endured, it is nature's way of nurturing us, pausing us, giving us time to heal and come to terms with loss.

Dying Matters (4) is a coalition of individual and organisational members across England and Wales, which aims to help people talk more openly about dying, death and bereavement and to make plans for the end of life.

Death affects us all at some time in our lives. It is important for us all to get to know grieving and, in doing so, speak more freely and honestly about grief. Not doing so can result in the following:

- Our mind and body is interconnected, so keeping thoughts, feelings and emotions trapped in can cause physical and emotional stress and affect behaviour
- Relationships, family life and work can suffer
- We don't get the support we need so we don't feel supported
- We can feel alone, misunderstood, as if we are on the outside of life, looking in
- Episodes of anxiety, depression and other mental health issues can be pro-longed

In summary

1. Let's agree to use the D words when relating to death. This will help everybody and be especially beneficial for children and those on the autistic spectrum who can understand the meaning of the dictionary words but may not understand what the ambiguous phrases of 'passed away', 'gone' or 'lost' mean when used in the context of death/dying/deceased.
2. Let's start using the grieving words with family, friends, colleagues to let them know- 'I'm grieving', 'he's grieving', 'she's grieving', 'we're grieving', 'they're grieving'.
3. Let's not shy away from death and grieving

Turn to chapter 2 to learn the genuine reactions of grieving and how this looks and feels in your mind, body and behaviour.

Chapter 2 -
Genuine Reactions to Grief

You may be surprised to learn how many grief reactions there actually are and how they can bring about changes to your body (physical), your mind (mental/psychological) and feelings (emotions). Often clients are reassured when I show them this list of grief reactions.

Take 32 year old Sonya, who was relieved when she saw 'lack of concentration' and 'forgetful' on the list as she'd been worrying she was starting with dementia.

Sonya felt she was 'going mad' or 'losing it', before she saw the list so was reassured to know these are all normal reactions to grief.

The list contains 3 columns:

1. Feelings/emotions
2. Psychological/mental reactions
3. Physical reactions

They are displayed randomly and not in any order.

Some are more common than others.

Some can be linked to other conditions.

There are 24 words/phrases in each of my columns.

72 grieving thoughts, feelings, emotions, physical reactions for you to contend with.

"Unless we agree to suffer we cannot be free from suffering"

D T SUZUKI

Just like Suzuki above, I believe that you have to come to an understanding that some of these many reactions will cause you some pain, anguish or distress and are to be expected in some way or another and at some time on your grieving pathway.

Take a look at the list, you may want to mark a cross against those you can relate to:

Mental

Feelings
Fear
Panic
Relief
Vulnerable
Lonely
Overwhelmed
Sadness
Freedom
Hope
Upset
Bewildered
Hurt
Afraid
Frustrated
Dread
Feeling of unreality
Low self-esteem
Loss of purpose
Incompetence
Pity
Love
Hate
Madness
Unfairness

Psychological
Distress
Despair
Numbness
Anger
Blame
Guilt
Hallucinations
- seeing, feeling,
hearing things
Denial
Confusion
Restlessness
Lack of concentration
Low mood
Irritable
Agitated
Depression
Anxiety
Apathy
Wanting to be alone
Meaning of death/
loss of faith
Questioning yourself
Yearning/searching
Forgetting how he/
she looked/sounded
Forgetful
Inability to trust

Physical

Body
Crying
Shock
Pain
Palpitations
Shortness of breath or
Shallow breathing
Sleep disturbance -
sleeping too much or
too little
Dry mouth/dry cough
Headache/Migrane/
Twitchy eye
Stomach upset
Weight loss/gain
Fatigue - loss of
energy
Menstruation changes
Loss of interest in life
Symptoms of the
deceased
Tight chested
Blood pressure
changes
Hair loss
Indigestion
Nausea/vomiting
Recurrent infections
e.g. colds, cold sores
Dreams/nightmares
Present condition
worsens e.g. eczema/
asthma
A need to swallow
often
Loss of libido/Erectile
Dysfunction

Did you know there were so many, how many of these have you had?

Have you experienced any others?

Some are more common than others, not sleeping very well, for example, is a common complaint.

Sonya admitted she was having trouble sleeping, waking up multiple times in the night, thoughts whirring round and round in her mind. This lack of sleep that affected Sonya's emotional, physical and mental state can have a knock on effect with relationships, work and most likely memory and concentration too. Hence the lack of concentration and forgetfulness Sonya had related to on the 'reactions' list.

Less common can be any kind of sensory hallucination, such as a feeling of heaviness on your bed sheet as though their body weight is laid on the bed with you, which can feel upsetting or frightening to experience.

If you have ever suffered with stress, anxiety or depression then you may recognise some of the symptoms listed as they can be very similar, if not the same.

Sometimes, these are not attributed to grief reactions as they can appear at a time when you don't associate them with your grieving, that is weeks or months after your loss/death was experienced. (It is worth remembering this and checking in with yourself to establish if this may be the case for you – if so, a bit of self-care may be required which I cover in Chapter 5). Sonya's husband had died six months earlier so she assumed her symptoms were not related to her grief; discovering they were felt somehow better. Realising where they sprang from gave her the chance to address her symptoms, cope with them and deal with them differently.

After years of studying grieving both personally and professionally I've come to the conclusion that:

Grieving is the process of actively working through a genuine reaction of very intense thoughts, feelings and behaviours that you experience as part of the natural end to someone/ something in your life.

Your reaction to death (or loss), when someone (or something), leaves your life, for what-ever reason, is a reflex response, a spontaneous effect.

You genuinely feel the powerful effect on your mind and body. It is not faked and you really feel the intense, deep emotions come over you.

Your goodbye is the end, just as in a natural cycle of life - birth, growth, reproduction and death, and this end is the natural farewell.

If you like an acronym to remember what GRIEVING and GRIEF are, here are mine:

Genuine Reaction In Experiencing Very Intense Natural Goodbyes

And

Genuine Reaction In Experiencing Feelings (mind and body)

When Jenny's daughter died she felt she had pushed her emotions away, choosing to keep herself busy to take her mind off them instead of allowing herself time and space to notice her thoughts and feelings and sit with them. Sadly, two years on, she was only beginning to deal with her grief. If only she had allowed the flow of grieving to occur naturally after her daughter's death.

Nature can help, we can trust the air we breathe, the earth we walk on, the water we drink, the sun that shines. Nature knows exactly what needs to be done, when and in what order. The trees know when to shed their leaves in autumn to make way for new leaves in the Spring.

If we stay in tune with our intrinsic nature, the nature that is inside us, then we can stay in harmony with both nature and our true selves. We can consider our own natural rhythms and ask ourselves 'what is good for me, right now?'

If we do as intended, relaxing into it and allowing ourselves to feel, then the flow of grieving just happens, so why not turn towards it not against and let it happen naturally (5). It is valuable time to nourish your mind and body and part of your protection for your health and wellbeing. It is a necessary important space to process the details of your loss, to miss and remember them –to grieve them. I will cover how you can do this in more detail in chapter 6.

Although grieving the loss of a loved one is natural, grief, as I'm sure you're aware, is a complex thing. It takes many forms and nearly always lasts longer than one might expect (6).

How you will react to grief cannot be predicted. It is important therefore to familiarise yourself with the kinds of intense thoughts, feelings and reactions which a state of grief can cause. Forewarned is forearmed, as they say, so looking closely at responses to grief now will help you cope when they do occur.

Sometimes bereavement happens when you are already under stress from other life events such as redundancy, a house move or a new relationship beginning. This intensifies your grief reactions.

> Josh's mum died unexpectedly during his final year of university when he was already feeling the pressure of writing up his dissertation. The additional layer of grief mixed in with his already fragile state of mind felt too hard to bear.

Here are some of the common grieving thoughts/feelings, which can be deep, passionate, powerful and serious – see how many you can relate to:

Despair

- Crying more than usual
- Crying for no specific reason
- Crying for the least little thing – not something that would usually upset you
- Unable to hold back the tears at unexpected times and in unexpected places- food shopping for example or whilst at work but when you weren't consciously thinking of your loved one
- No crying – just sitting staring into space
- Unable to cry but want to
- Just sitting in silence, alone and/or in company – wanting to be alone
- No conversation in you
- Feeling empty
- Feeling unworthy/unloved
- Unable to move or to do much
- Disengaged from life, wanting to run away, escape from how you feel

Anger

- Feeling angry about 'stuff'
- Feeling angry for the least little thing
- Feeling jealous of other people's family situation
- Thinking bad thoughts of other's loved ones, sometimes wishing they were dead, so they'd know how you feel right now

- Feeling like others just don't know how you feel right now
- Feeling like you don't understand yourself or that others don't understand you
- Angry that other family members are not crying/ grieving like you
- Feeling mad when people enjoy themselves or laugh
- Feeling very cross about life and the meaning of life

Guilt/blame

- Feeling like you don't understand anything anymore
- Feeling like you can't laugh as laughing makes you feel guilty and disrespectful
- Blaming someone/anyone
- Blaming yourself for …
- Feeling so guilty for …
- Feeling like you weren't prepared for it?
- Using 'they' a lot in conversation and thinking 'they' could/should have done more, blaming the doctors, nurses etc., even family members

Depressive type thoughts

- Not washing, showering, bathing enough, not caring about your personal hygiene
- Not getting dressed every day or caring about how you look
- Not cooking for yourself/others/not eating balanced/ healthy meals
- Feeling very moody – up and down
- Avoiding friends and family
- Avoiding dealing with bills, paperwork, household jobs etc
- Work related issues, time off, poor performance, distancing from colleagues

- Unable to concentrate
- Unable to ask for help
- Unable to explain yourself
- Feeling like you're stuck in some kind of time warp
- Feeling like time is standing still for you while the world around you continues as normal
- Feeling like you'll never 'get over this'
- Feeling like you'll never be able to accept what's happened
- Feeling like you won't be able to move on
- Feeling like you'll feel this way forever

Concerning thoughts/actions – (may need to seek help with these)

- Reckless behaviour -feeling like you want to do dangerous things/get your adrenalin pumping/risky sexual encounters/driving recklessly for example
- Drinking alcohol – too much-too often
- Taking drugs/painkillers to numb the pain
- Escapism – pretend you're somebody else/want to be somebody else/don't want to be you right now
- Feeling so down and so low in mood that life no longer feels like living

Anxiety and worry are very common reactions and can show in a number of ways during grief:

You worry...

You can't stop your worrying	You may be next, what if you die now, suddenly, what if you become poorly
About who to ask for help or if you'll become a burden to others	You will forget them, their voice, their face
What people think - of you, how you're coping, judging how you're being	How you will cope on your own, you don't know where you keep things in the house like the light bulbs, the paperwork, etc
You won't know how to do things, like the children's school stuff for example	You just won't cope

In summary:

- Being prepared for some of the many reactions you may experience is a good start to understanding grieving but this will not stop you experiencing them. It can, however, lessen their hold, intensity and duration at times.

- You can never fully prepare for grief because every death/loss, circumstance and relationship will be different and our grief reaction different too.

- Knowing that what you are experiencing is 'normal' is reassuring and if you know what to expect then you can figure out how to cope.

- Some reactions only occur in the early days of grieving, Some come later on when you may not expect them, Some are with you all the time that you are grieving, Some come and go… come and go… come and go…in 'waves of emotion'

- Trust in your connection to nature.

- You can start getting to know yourself and think about your own self-help remedies. You can read more about helping yourself in chapters 5, 6, and 7.

Learning what grieving is, is a first step. Just knowing what genuine reactions to expect from a natural goodbye can take away the fear of feeling out of control. Some reactions can get better with a bit of tender loving care: looking after yourself; eating properly; resting (if you're not sleeping properly); managing anxiety/stress; and giving yourself time to grieve. All of which I will cover in the next chapters.

Chapter 3 -
Change, Loss and Grieving

When someone we love dies, we say goodbye to life as it was and our lives change forever. It can be a huge change. It may only be a small change. Either way, we have to learn to cope with it and adjust to it, as our lives will never be the same again.

Loss too causes changes to feelings, behaviours and lifestyles in much the same way as grief as we saw in Chapter 2. As well as suffering the death of a spouse, partner, child, family member, friend, colleague, neighbour, pet, there may be other losses which you may not have associated with grief reactions before. For example:

* A special person missing from your life
* Miscarriage/Fertility
* Loss of health/personal injury/hearing/sight
* Redundancy/change of job/status/manager/colleagues/ change of responsibilities at work
* Change in finances/debt
* Divorce/separation/relationship breakdown
* House repossession/house move/home broken into
* Children left home –empty nest

- Retirement
- Friendship ended
- Failed exams
- Identity

You may have experienced other personal losses that are not on the above list. Have a think about these and how you may have been affected and how you coped. Maybe you can see similarities to the way you feel now you are grieving.

As we saw in Chapter 2, you can be affected by more than one loss/death at the same time and this can be especially difficult to deal with, pushing some people to breaking point.

It can therefore be reassuring to know there are differing theories or models which can help us to better understand the roots and the range of these reactions. Each model offers us a different lens through which to approach grief. It is entirely up to you which you prefer or relate to. I'll briefly explain them now.

The five stages

Elisabeth Kubler-Ross, one well-known expert on change (7) identifies five stages of grief. You can be in any stage at any time, you can be in different stages at different times, you can go back to some of the stages you have been in before. Each stage can last any length of time and can exist side by side with another stage:

Denial, Anger, Bargaining, Depression & Acceptance

Here's an example of what each of Kubler Ross's five stages of grief might look like for you:

Denial – This can't be happening, I can't believe it, not to me, not again, it's not real

Anger – Why me/him/her? It's not fair, No I can't accept this!

Bargaining – I'll do anything if only I could see him/her again, if I had just had more time I could have...

Depression – What's the point?, I'm so sad, why bother with anything?

Acceptance – I'll just have to get on with this, it's going to be OK

Remember, the natural grieving process has no order, it all takes place over several months.

Other theorists have since argued that there is a period often referred to as **restoration or adjustment,** the sixth stage. Restoring and rebuilding your life without your loved one can take some adjusting to but it is a necessary part of the process of grieving. I cover some of these elements in Chapter 7, learning to live with grief.

The dual process model

From their research into grief Stroebe and Schut (8) believe that grief operates in two ways and people naturally switch from one to the other as they grieve. It is called the dual process model because two different processes are happening.

1. Loss orientation: this is the dimension linked to the grief, the loss, sadness, pain, yearning, looking at old photographs of the deceased, the things that make you think about your loved one.

2. Restoration orientation: the changes brought with loss, learning to do new tasks (which the deceased used to do) as well as tending to your everyday chores and dealing with daily aspects of life.

What does this oscillation between the two modes look like in practice? Imagine you clean your car in the morning and are distracted from your grief - this is restoration orientation. Then you hear a song on the radio which reminds you of your loved one and makes you cry – this is loss orientation. After crying for a while you then think 'right, I need to go food shopping!' and move back to restoration orientation.

Stroebe and Schut argue that ignoring your emotions or distracting yourself from your grief is a natural way of coping. Think of it as 'time off' from your grief. If you stay in loss mode for too long, you could end up not looking after yourself or getting on with daily life. Likewise, if you deny the reality of the death and avoid the restoration you can inhibit or delay your grief.

This model allows for healthy doses of both loss and restoration and allows you to live your daily life as a changed person without being consumed by the grieving you are facing.

Tonkins model

This model is useful for those whose grief and pain is as bad as ever and has never really gone away, time has not healed the wounds. Tonkin (9) suggests for some, you do not move on from grief, but grow your life around it. This theory can be helpful as it relieves the expectation that grief is temporary and should go away.

It is sometimes referred to as the 'fried egg model' with grief as the yolk in the middle of the egg and life as the surrounding egg white. In the early days of grief, there may only be a yolk and no white and this represents how your grief consumes your whole life. In the following days, months however the yolk remains the same size but the white grows bigger, representing your life growing around your grief, with your grief staying much the same.

This model can be helpful for those who feel a sense of disloyalty to the deceased and wish to continue their bond by integrating the loss into their life.

In summary:

• There are lots of other models of grief but these three are my particular favourites and the ones I most often refer clients to. I hope they help you.

Chapter 4 -
Your Goodbyes

To re-cap on what you've learnt so far, death and grieving are difficult to talk about, there are many genuine reactions that involve thoughts, feelings, and actions with a number of theoretical models to explain this. But there is still another vital aspect to consider and that is YOU.

You are unique and your life story is individual to you. Similarly, the way that you grieve will be different to others too; everyone grieves in their own way and at their own pace. Your life is made up of a number of factors which all determine how your grieving can be affected and each of them can have a different impact on how this will be. This is why every time you experience a death, you will have a different grief reaction. Just as no two deaths are the same, no two grieving episodes will be the same either.

Let's have a look at some of these factors:

- Your **identity** – who you are, your sexuality, your gender, your birth details
- Your **beliefs** – religion/spirituality
- Your **values** –what you consider important to you- love, money, family, work, home, possessions

- Your **ethics** – what you consider to be right and wrong
- Your **history** – your age, your past life, your life story
- Your **family** – your role, status, where you are placed in the family tree
- Your **family dynamics** – single parent, blended family, step, half-brothers/sisters
- Your **friends** – how many you have, how long you've known them, their role
- Your **relationships** – single, married, partner, lover, friends, pets
- Your **life experience** –what you've done, what you know, your career, your hobbies, your age
- Your **support network** – family, friends, colleagues, neighbours, online acquaintances, others
- Your **coping skills** – how you deal with setbacks, any previous experience of dealing with stress, anxiety, depression etc., your outlook on life, your expectations, your mind-set
- Your **situation** –what the loss is, when it happened, how it happened, where you're at right now, are you dealing with any other stressful circumstances as well as this –if so how many-are you already struggling before this happened?
- Your **death related issues** – funeral arrangements, Last will and testament, choice of executor, assets, possessions, heir looms –can cause conflict & memories of the deceased

This is why death and loss affect us all differently and no two people will experience the same loss in the same way. Even within the same family, each member will be grieving differently due to all the factors mentioned above. It's worth remembering this as it can feel very different when you're in the middle of this.

When Alex's Dad died, he grieved privately, no outward show of emotions, no crying in front of the family. He just quietly visited his dad's grave every week by himself, to cry there. His sister was enraged by her brother's apparent lack of feeling. Didn't he care? Why wasn't he upset? Why wasn't he crying like she was? She didn't realise they were both grieving in their own different ways.

It is this difference that needs to be considered when coping with YOUR loss. It is best not to compare your goodbyes to the goodbyes of others.

Your personal story - how you knew the person, how you feel about them, what they mean to you, what role they held in your life - will be different to another's experience of loss.

Ali was struggling to come to terms with the death of his best 'friend'. This friendship was a secret Ali kept from his family as it did not align with their values and beliefs. This made him question his identity and his role in the family status. He was the eldest son, the strong, capable, dependable one and now he was a broken man but nobody knew why. To him, his situation was unbearable, his support network limited and his future bleak.

It could be that your loss represents the following to you:

- Loss of your soul mate, your hopes, your dreams, your future together
- Loss of family member, change in family dynamics, change in family arrangements; birthday, Christmas, celebrations
- Your companion/buddy/friend to go places with/do things with
- Someone you could trust/confide in/someone who knew you inside out
- Someone you cared for/looked after/your sense of purpose
- Your beloved pet
- Your DIY expert/jobs around the house person/ household bills/paperwork/finances person
- Your holiday companion
- Someone to have a drink with/lunch with/make meals for
- Your gardener/cleaner
- Your social organiser
- Your fitness companion, someone you played sports with
- Your teacher/mentor/voice of wisdom/voice of reason, go to person in a crisis

There will be many more roles I am sure you can think of…

You not only lose the person but everything else they represented and this is why it is important to identify their role(s) as the loss can affect different aspects of your life, in different ways.

Jan and her work colleague Vicky were pregnant at the same time, they hardly knew one another outside work but were planning on spending their maternity leave together-walks, baby groups, play areas etc. Then the unthinkable happened, tragically, at 20+ weeks Vicky's baby died and a week later, she died too of cancer of the womb. Jan's strong grief reaction took her by surprise. At Vicky's funeral she let out an audible sob, which had mourners turning around and taking her arm to steady her. Maybe those mourners wondered who she was and why she had reacted in this way. Of course, they did not know the plans that Jan and Vicky had made for their friendship and their babies. Now all this was gone and Jan was deeply upset.

As well as missing the person, you miss these other things too, all they represented in your life and these can be so, so tough to cope with too.

No matter what your relationship to the person, you can be affected in many ways.

Even if a relationship was conflictual or fraught with difficulties, you can still grieve. In fact, sometimes you may grieve more. You can find yourself grieving for missed opportunities; for the 'if only' times or for not spending 'enough' time together.

Understanding all of this is crucial, so you know why you feel this way and what you may need help and support with.

To help you through this you may need to have extra help. Jan did, and she spoke to a counsellor.

You may have to learn to do some things for yourself now or you may need to ask for extra help from others.

- Asking for help can all be very daunting especially when you may not be feeling your best and you are feeling very vulnerable.
- Some think they need to sort themselves out first before seeking help but this I find to be a delaying tactic.
- In my experience, your support circle do generally want to help and would be all too pleased to do something to help you, however small or trivial you think this may be.
- It is fine to ask for help. It is a sign of strength not weakness to ask for what you need and to accept any support offered. Helping is often two-way, the one giving the help can feel as much benefit as the one receiving.
- Friends and family often do not know what to say or how 'to be' around you whilst you grieve, so providing any kind of practical help feels like they are 'being there for you'. Let them help you.
- It may be easier to write down what you need help with so you can say specifically what will help you and what you need help with.
- Sometimes it is the small tasks which seem hardest to do alone, such as:

    ⇨ Dealing with the post or any legal, financial and banking matters
    ⇨ Making phone calls and/or letters to people/ companies can be daunting
    ⇨ Sorting through belongings can be traumatic
    ⇨ Household matters can feel huge
    ⇨ Food shopping can be a dread

Perhaps there are other things you are struggling with, can anyone else help?

In summary:

- You are an individual and every individual loss is different for you and others.
- There are many factors to consider and to work through.
- You may need some help working through these.

Chapter 5 - How to Cope

Coping with the intense reactions in the early days, weeks and months after a death or a significant loss or change may feel impossible. But taking time with your healing will mean that someday you will hurt less. You will learn to cope with the raw and powerful thoughts and feelings as this chapter explains.

Quite simply, it takes time. You need to permit yourself to heal slowly and take the time to miss your loved one. Bowlby, a famous grief theorist, said it is the yearning for the impossible, the self-indulgent anger, the powerless weeping, the fear at the prospect of loneliness, the deserving pleading for sympathy and support, that are the feelings we need to express or discover for the first time in grief, in order to work through it (10).

These are, of course, strong words, with which you may or may not agree. But there is one clear definite: no one else can do your grieving for you and you have to reconcile yourself to this, however daunting or difficult it may seem.

Sadly, you cannot bypass the grieving process. You have to grieve in some shape or form. This personal process has been likened by some to the transformation of a caterpillar, growing whilst cocooned in its chrysalis.

'Left to nature, it will spend time in its cocoon doing what it needs to do and when it is ready it will struggle free from its chrysalis, to emerge as a beautiful butterfly.

However, if anyone tries to prevent this struggle, cut the chrysalis open before the caterpillar is ready, it will not grow and survive.'
(11)

Healing, from grieving, can be a struggle which takes time. Take it slowly, one hour, one day at a time, knowing that you can live and find chinks of light in this darkness.

Time itself does not automatically heal your pain but remember, the way you feel now will not last forever. Grief changes over time. It helps if you are aware of the intense feelings of the natural goodbyes, work with them, understand them and recognise that your moods and behaviour will be affected by them.

Give yourself permission to grieve.

Loss of control

We all know that when we have to adapt to change – be it at work or in our personal lives – that change can make us feel like we are losing control. Grief can make you feel that way too, which can be very frightening.

It is also very normal to feel as though you are going backwards with your grieving feelings, just when you thought you were starting to move forwards. This too can be deeply disorienting.

Don't panic, Sue Morris (12) suggests an effective way of taking back some of this control by allowing yourself a set amount of time each day to grieve and using this set time to do your remembering.

If this method does not work for you, you could choose to grieve in your own way and take control in other areas of your life.

There are a number of things which can help you cope, some you may already practice or have come across before. Nevertheless, they may be worth trying again. Remember, you are in control of your own well-being and only you will know what works for you and what you feel like doing on any given day.

Here's what I've seen work well for my clients:

Treat every day as it comes

No two days will be the same. Do what feels right for you.

Keep to your normal routine as much as possible.

You may not feel like it, but it is important to do a bit of something every day. Even if it means just getting up, showering/bathing, getting dressed and getting yourself a bit of something to eat and drink, watching TV. Everyday tasks, nothing fancy.

Relaxation time

It is important to make time to slow down and spend some time doing nothing much. Have an occasional day staying in your nightwear/lounge wear, allowing yourself a day off, giving yourself time to come round and spending the day relaxing.

Be aware that, staying in bed for days on end however, will not help in the long run and will only prolong your pain.

Private time

It could be that you find it easier to grieve alone and privately. Beware though, never expressing your grief externally can be emotionally devastating. Carol Staudacher (13) explains that this emotional silence can cause some difficulties which you may want to avoid. Finding a safe space, and time, where you don't feel embarrassed or self-conscious, to let go of your emotions is essential to your grieving.

So if you prefer to grieve privately and alone you could choose to visit the grave, or your special memorial place, and express your grief outwardly by talking to your loved one and crying whilst there for example.

Fear of 'breaking down'

'I don't want to breakdown' is a phrase I'm sure most people have heard a grieving person say at some time or another. It nearly always refers to some kind of crying. Trying to be 'the strong one' in the family, the one 'holding it all together' can also be linked to this fear. As Cruse Bereavement says, 'crying is part of recovery'. (14). Crying is a natural response to pain so any form of crying; sobbing, weeping, snivelling, or being teary can be very therapeutic for the mind and body.

Crying at any time during your grieving is normal. It does not mean that you are 'losing it'.

Remember you are important to other people

You may not feel like caring for yourself right now, but others care about you and may be finding it difficult to express this for fear of upsetting you or saying the wrong thing at the wrong time.

Let your feelings out, don't bottle your feelings for too long

If you're feeling overwhelmed talking can help. Talking helps to ease the pain, and helps you make sense of things. If you can't face talking to family/friends, it could be a work colleague, an acquaintance, a friendly face at your local, someone at your place of worship or a complete stranger. You just need one person who is willing to listen.

Charities and voluntary organisations are always willing to listen and I've listed a few at the back of this book, likewise your GP will be able to support you and refer you to an appropriate therapy for you. Trained therapists offer a safe environment where you can offload thoughts and feelings and work through them together and without judgement. All counselling service are confidential, can be offered face to face on a one to one session, over the telephone, via Skype/Teams/Zoom or you could choose a group session, with others. What-ever you feel will work best for you, that's what matters.

Writing

An excellent alternative to talking is writing. Transferring your thoughts onto paper is such an effective way of taking them off your mind, helping you make more sense of them when they are written down. Don't know the science behind how it works, but trust me, it works.

Writing can be very therapeutic, be it lists, letters, notes, diaries, cards, messages, rhymes, poems, or songs.

Coping with Guilt/Shame/Blame

If you are feeling distressed with a strong sense of 'I should have' or 'if only' or reliving a scene over and over again, wishing you could change it, then it may help to try writing to the person missing from your life. Write from your heart and be sure to include:

• What you feel happened, the facts of what happened and how you feel affected

Please do not punish yourself for something that cannot be changed. It is what it is, no amount of self-torture will change the situation. If you want you could think of their perspective and see if you can reply as if they were speaking through you. What might they say to you, how might they reply, would they be likely to accept your explanation/apology now they know your side of the story, would they want you to torment yourself in this way?

Anger management

A natural response to loss can be anger and these feelings can be very intense and very scary. Coping with any raging feelings can be difficult to live with and control. Some positive ways to deal with anger is often by using physical exercise, where you can physically work out your angry emotion, housework, DIY, gardening, sport etc.

Others find it helpful to channel anger towards a good cause or charity to help make a difference or campaign for a change in a law for example.

Or you can simply do any of the following techniques often used to help children (15) but just as effective for adults too:

- Write down your anger –then enjoy the satisfaction of tearing it up and throwing it away
- punch a pillow/cushion
- stomp, walk really fast or run

Just a word of caution for writing when angry. If you plan to send your writing to someone living, never send or act on it that same day. Wait until tomorrow and re-read it, how you're feeling today, can feel very different in the morning.

Busyness

Keeping busy to avoid dealing with your pain can help in the short and medium-term, but long term this can start to have a negative effect on your mental wellbeing. Try not to overcrowd your life (16), accept some invitations and offers of socialising whilst also keeping some time for yourself.

Living space

Try to keep the house/living space under control (17) and keep doing the basics but take it steady and do a bit at a time. As they say, a little goes a long way and a tidy house is a tidy mind and this will help when trying to deal with the psychological effects of your grief. A cluttered, dirty living space will only add to any negative feelings. The Japanese consider cleaning as a practice to nurture the mind, not a chore, but to eliminate mental gloom.

Exercise

Any form of exercise will be good for you – housework, gardening, DIY, walking, jogging, swimming, cycling, yoga, dancing, even singing.

Emotionally, it will make you feel better and it will also tire you a little physically so this can improve your sleeping.

Sleeping

You may be having trouble falling asleep or waking often in the night. You may also experience more dreams or nightmares. It is normal but can be hard to live with as the tiredness can affect your mood and how you feel, making you feel worse.

Try to avoid any stimulants at least one hour before bedtime; caffeine, using mobile phones, IPad, laptops etc.

- Keep your bedroom cool
- Clutter free if possible
- Putting a couple of drops of lavender oil on your pillow can help relax you
- Listening to relaxing music or a guided meditation can help too

If you wake in the night, read for a while or just get up or write down your thoughts and get them off your mind, instead of having them going round and round in your head.

If you are really struggling see your GP/pharmacist who may be able to prescribe/recommend something to help.

Pause

If you get upset whilst doing something or you experience an unpleasant or difficult thought, **just pause.** Let the moment happen, notice where you may be feeling the unpleasantness – is it in your head, chest, stomach or somewhere else, see if you can be with the sensations without reacting. Feel it, stay with it, let the tears flow and feel the sadness. A wave of emotion is often how this can be best described. Just like the sea, waves come and then go. Let it be, this too shall pass.

When you're ready, carry on as you were OR stop completely and try again another time, when you feel able to.

Breathe

Breathing is so natural to us that you probably take it for granted, yet when you get in tune with your breath it can be a really good indicator for how you are feeling. How does your breath feel now? Is it in your throat, chest or stomach? Does it feel panicky, shallow, rough and short or is it deep, smooth and relaxed? Learning how to breathe deeply, slowly, mindfully (in the present moment) and meditatively is so important and beneficial. Research has found it has life changing benefits:

- You can live longer
- You can ease anxiety, depression, stress
- You can feel more positive
- You can lower your blood pressure
- You can cope better with pain
- You can boost your immune system which helps with colds, flu and other diseases

All so helpful when grieving.

If you want to find peace in this frantic world (18), **then follow this 60 second meditation:**

1. Sit as straight and tall as you can with your feet flat on the floor
2. Lower your gaze or close your eyes
3. Notice your breath as you breathe in (lower belly inflates) and breathe out (lower belly deflates). It can be helpful to place your left hand on your heart space and your right hand on your lower belly so you can feel your right hand moving out as you breathe in and moving down as you breathe out.
4. If your mind wanders (which it will) just re-start noticing your breath again as it flows into your body and out again. (It can be easier to visualise your breath as a colour or smoke so you can see it flowing in and out).
5. Repeat this technique until you feel calm

Practicing deep breathing is free and always available, anytime, anywhere, it really is the best medicine. As well as this abdominal breathing, there are lots more techniques to try such as alternate nostril breathing and square breaths.

To get you started you may prefer to listen to a guided meditation or CD or use a book or seek out a good meditation/ yoga teacher.

Personally, meditation is now one of my preferred ways of coping with my grief. After years of resisting trying this, I have truly enjoyed exploring the healing power of breath work and only wish I'd started this sooner. I firmly believe breath work/meditation should be taught in school.

For anxious and depressive thoughts, try and stay in the present moment

For your health and wellbeing it is best to try and stay in the present moment, nowadays this is often referred to as *mindfulness*. Easy to say, but often harder to do.

When grieving it's natural for your thoughts to focus on looking forward and what your future will be now without your loved one. However, too many of these type of thoughts can cause anxiety which can cause a panicky feeling and shallow breathing/shortness of breath. They tend to start with a 'what if', which is a worrying thought. There is an old saying along the lines of "if you look for worry, it will find you", which is very true in my opinion. So, try to stop a 'what if' thought as soon as it pops into your head and replace it with 'I will deal with whatever happens if it happens'. Tell yourself 'I've got this!' Should haves and could dos tend to come with some kind of guilt attached so drop these too and say "I'd like to" instead, so much softer and more forgiving, gives the intention you want to, but may not be able to right now.

Likewise, if you tend to spend too much time looking back at what was, clinging to the past, this can be linked to depressive thoughts. Whilst grieving involves elements of looking back and remembering, which I will cover in Chapter 6, the key thing is the amount of time you're spending in this state of mind.

You may recognise this for yourself, or a friend/family member may notice when you're spending too much time in either one of these thought patterns. I once read somewhere:

'*No time like the present–*

A human mind is a wandering mind and a wandering mind is an unhappy mind.

Be mindful of what's going on right now.

Pay attention to what you can smell, see and hear and how you feel.

If your thoughts wander to the past or future, gently guide your thoughts back to the present'.

When your mind starts wandering in a negative way, try focussing on something practical you can do right now. Meditate/practice your breathing/relaxation techniques, do some exercise, tidy your living space, water the plants, go for a walk, clean the car, dust the windowsills, prepare a meal or wash the pots for example, or write your thoughts down to bring you back to the present moment, back to the here and now.

In summary:

- You may recognise some of these suggestions as the restoration mode from Chapter 3. What I'd like you to take from this chapter is the knowledge that you can learn when you're starting to feel out of control and cope with it when you do.
- Remember, we all grieve differently - in our own way and in our own time. There is no right or wrong way to grieve, but sadly no-one else can grieve for you, it is something you must do yourself.
- Feeling out of control is normal and there are different coping strategies to help you take back this control.

It is ok to have help, be open to suggestions, look for alternative ways and keep doing what feels right for you.

- In addition to my self-help sources of coping, widen your search and gain other perspectives, not just mine. Try something new, something you may not have considered before. Sometimes something new is needed, a new approach, something different.

Chapter 6 -
Different Ways of Remembering

We know death is difficult to talk about. There are lots of genuine reactions to deal with and every goodbye is different. There are, as we've seen, many things we can do to cope during these intense times. I don't say this lightly; I know how hard it is to say goodbye to someone you love.

However, grieving is about remembering. Not just the bad times and the bad memories but all the special moments you spent together, the treasured times, the good times.

Whilst it may feel painful to think about your loved one, it is a necessary part of the grieving process.

Healing happens as you begin to let your feelings happen.

Remembering allows them to live on, not in the physical sense but in your heart, soul and mind.

Some refer to this as keeping a continuing bond, where you find ways to keep their memory alive. You can adjust and redefine your relationship with the person throughout your life by remembering them thus continuing the bond with them (19).

Here are some ways to continue remembering your loved one; some you may have not considered as ways of grieving but they are. There are ways to suit every one of us that reflect our style, our personality or that of your loved one. Some you may consider because you know that's what your loved one would like so it's another way of honouring them. The process of planning them as well as doing them may give you comfort and pleasure which is well deserved considering the emotional turmoil you will have endured so far.

Remember there is no time limit to your grieving so don't feel you have to rush and do them all immediately. Pace yourself. Do them as and when you're in the mood.

In a few months' time, you may find yourself re-visiting this list particularly if you've hit a rough patch. You can do these at any time.

Some you can do alone, some may need help from others or some you may just prefer to do with some company from friends/family for support. Take a look at them and choose the ones which fit best for you, some are really obvious and common but others not so much so:

Talking about your loved one is a way of remembering them:

- Using their name in conversation
- Using their favourite sayings
- Referring to their likes and dislikes
- Recalling their sense of humour
- Retelling stories/times spent together
- Reminiscing about your memory of them

Talking to them:

- Greeting their photograph with a 'morning' or 'night-night' or a kiss
- Asking questions out loud is common too –'where did you keep the….?' For example
- Jon talks to his late wife whilst un-packing his food shopping, knowing she would not approve of his food choices!

Memorials:

- Grave/headstone/ashes
- Plant a tree/flowers/bush
- Roadside memorial- photograph, notes/messages, flowers, cuddly toy
- Bench/seat in favourite place
- Vase
- Statue
- Plaque
- Online tribute sites such as: Much loved.com (reference 20)
- Social media pages/blogs etc.

Ashes:

Decide what to do with their ashes in your own time, there is no rush, you can:

- Keep/store/display in a fancy container
- Scatter
- Bury
- Make them shiny in jewellery, glass and other ornaments

- Tattoo
- Search on the internet for things to do with cremated ashes for further ideas (21).

Belongings:

There is no right answer as to what to do with your loved one's belongings, nor is there no right time to deal with them. It is best to take your time to decide what is best for you, no need to rush this. You can choose to:

- Keep (as they are, some refer to this as a shrine).
- Wear a favourite item, jewellery for example can help you feel connected
- Give away - to family, friends, charity for example, so others can benefit.
- Sell
- Up-cycle
- Throw away
- Make your favourite items into; memory pillow, memory cushion, memory quilt, memory teddy bear. Search on the internet for more ideas on this...

Thinking of them is a way of remembering:

While you sit quietly you may want to remember the following types of thoughts of them:

- What was your relationship to them?
- How did you meet?
- How long have you known them?
- What did you like about them?
- What were their personal characteristics?
- What legacy will they leave behind?

- What memorable traits have they passed on?
- What habits did they have?
- What did they like to do?
- What hobbies?
- What made them laugh?
- What were their favourite TV programmes/films
- What music/bands did they like?
- What were their values and beliefs?
- What annoyed them?
- What were their favourite sayings?

Of course you can also use these prompts as conversation points too, choosing to share your thoughts with others. It could be that you or someone you know shares the same traits or habits and this can be both comforting or annoying, depending on your frame of mind and your perspective. Looks too are often used as a reference point and you'll often hear phrases like 'I can see your dad in him' or 'she looks just like your mum'.

Photographs:

- Boxing them away safely for now (or add to a memory box)
- Looking at them and reminisce either privately or with others
- Display and frame favourites
- Enlarge favourites, re-print on canvass, acrylic etc.
- Make albums, displays, digital albums, screen savers on mobile phone/laptop.

Music:

- Listen to your favourite songs which make you feel better or to songs which soothe, comfort and heal you.

- When you feel ready, try listening to songs that remind you of them, try to recall happy memories.
- Reading/understanding the lyrics —finding meaning, finding a connection to your loved one.
- Exploring different styles —classical, opera, rock, pop, jazz, RnB, Rap, Country
- Making new playlists in memory of your loved one.

Making a memory box:

Does not have to be a box, can also be a special place, suitcase, tin, drawstring bag, shoe box. You can decorate it if you want. You can choose to keep it secret or to share with others, it's entirely what works best for you.

Items you can include are:

- Jewellery
- Favourite DVD
- Glasses
- ID badge
- Do a drawing
- Cufflinks
- Favourite aftershave
- Recipe
- Letters
- Socks
- Toy
- Photos

- Mobile phone/voice message
- Watch
- Write a letter/poem
- Tie
- Shaving brush
- Favourite perfume
- Cards
- Scarf
- Ornament
- Cuddly toy

Anything which means something to you to remember the person by. If you do not have any of their possessions you can use items of your choosing which remind you of them.

Other ideas for remembering:

- Name a star
- Key ring
- Remembrance books
- Christmas tree bauble/decoration
- Fragrances
- Wear their jewellery
- Poems
- Make a salt/sand coloured jar
- Light a candle
- Flowers
- Any association of them such as food/smells/colours/ numbers
- Scrap book
- Technology – videos, voice mail, an App to record their voice
- Memory prompts such as favourite chair/cushion/ clothes
- Precious and semi-precious stones
- Remembering you stone/pebble, you can buy or collect from a beach, someone once told me the following:

  Smooth – to remind you that the pain will slide off one day
  Hard – you have a deep inner strength and the courage to grieve
  Lines – you have had a difficult journey, but one we all must take
  Indentations – detours we want to avoid, but needed to grow, move on
  Colours – reflect your own beauty and the beauty we see around us

Memorial Tattoo:

Remember someone you loved with a tattoo of your choice.

Spiritual:

* Find connection, hope, meaning, another alternative way:
* Visit a place of worship
* Find faith/religion
* Pray/meditate
* Visit a spiritual healer: Clairvoyant/Medium/Intuitive healer/Tarot cards healer
* Reiki/Reflexology

Counsellor/bereavement volunteer:

Talk over how you are feeling to a trained therapist, see the recommended list at the back of the book.

Join a charity of your choice or in memory of your loved one

* Volunteer
* Fund raise (for a cause)
* Contribute in some way

Sponsored events:

Take part or contribute in memory/honour of your loved one or just for the feel good factor.

Online/community support group:

As a support network, peer support or to meet like-minded people who may have suffered a similar loss to you, search the internet for credible support groups available.

Organ donation

For some, knowing you have saved the life of another can be a comfort and a source of remembrance.

Gratitude:

Being thankful for having known them and having them in your life. Thinking of good times and the memories you now have to treasure. Thoughts, sayings, practicalities, memorabilia, possessions, memories and suggestions for living your life and moving forward. Giving you hopes and dreams, what they would want for you, would they want you to be forever sad?

Poems:

Can be a source of comfort and inspiration for many. Here are some of my favourites for you to look up:

Miss Me – But Let Me Go by Mary Frye

Life Goes On by Joyce Grenfell (1910-1979)

She is gone (can be interchanged with He) by David Harkins

In summary:

- There are many ways to remember your loved one, either alone or with others
- Memorials, ashes and belongings are perhaps the most obvious that are done collectively, but not always, there may only be you and that's ok too.
- Do the ones which will bring you some comfort, peace and joy
- Remembering is an important part of your grieving pathway

Chapter 7 -
Living with Grief

Throughout this book you've learned a bit more about what grieving is, the differing ways of coping and remembering your loved one. Now, it's time to think about how you can learn to live with your grief.

I'm sure you already know lots of people who are living with their grief and maybe you've never really considered how they've managed to do this.

If you know someone who's had a recent bereavement, try asking them. Find out what helped them cope. Unfortunately, there is no magic cure. For me, it's a matter of doing all of the things I've suggested so far in this book.

If we think back to Chapter 3 and the three different models of grief, you may have already found that one in particular resonated with you. Maybe it was the Tonkins' model suits you best and you can see the possibility of growing your life around your grief. No matter which model you relate to (and there are many others), the reality is, life as you know it, will never be the same.

This reality can be so hard to bear. You can wish, pray, plead and yearn for their return but it will never be. It is the finality of this fact for many feels so brutal.

Kubler-Ross, in her five stages of grief, refers to this as acceptance and I'm sure some well-meaning family and friends of yours have hinted at this too —saying things like: there's nothing you can do about it, you'll just have to accept it or you're just going to have to get on with it.

Margaret, 85 years old, after the death of her friend said 'you just get used to it'.

I think a softer, more positive and do-able approach is to say:

'I'm learning to adjust to my life without......'.

Don't get me wrong, saying this and doing this may not always be easy and some days you'll feel just as raw as you first did but if you take it day by day it will be more bearable.

Remember the way you feel now is temporary and will fade.

As the grieving pattern has no order and does not follow a logical process, you will have ups and downs. This is normal.

Two different authors I've come across have referenced thoughts from Dr Viktor Frankl, an Austrian psychiatrist (22 &23):

> Thought number one: *The purpose of life is to suffer well, which means going down into pain, owning it, not running from it but sitting with it and then you will find meaning from it.*
>
> Thought number two: *'Can we say yes to life in spite of everything?' even in the most miserable conditions, life is meaningful. The human capacity can creatively turn life's negative aspects into something positive or constructive.*

With this in mind, keep using the taking control coping techniques in chapter 5 to help you as you go along. You may need to try out the ones you have avoided so far to get you through a rough patch or tough time, you never know, they may be the ones which you need right now.

Also keep using the different ways to remember suggested in Chapter 6.

Learning how to be and live your life without your loved one, is all part of your grieving, which can take time, patience and understanding. Life continues without your loved one and you can learn to re-adjust, be happy and grow a new but different life. Loving and being loved again is not being disloyal to your loved one.

I found a simple happiness formula, which is: Having something to do + something to love + something to look forward to = happiness (24).

Below are 40 suggestions which incorporate every aspect of the happiness formula to help you heal your mind, body and soul.

Weave these things into your life, go back to an old hobby or try something new, add to your calendar, make a spreadsheet, keep coming back to this list, weeks, months after if you need to as a reminder of what there is out there to try:

1. Reading – fact, fiction, self- help
2. Yoga – excellent to heal the mind and body, this ancient practice has proved its benefits over thousands of years and really can help you to cope with stress and emotion.
3. Writing to heal, letters, poems, rhymes, books, diary
4. Meditating
5. Exercising –swim, run, cycle, dance, golf
6. Fresh air, get outdoors or open a window/sit by a window
7. Walking
8. Being in nature –can make you feel nurtured, all the wonderful things to be thankful for and enjoy; lakes, rivers, streams, oceans, mountains, fields, flowers can make us feel nourished. Try star gazing or forest bathing.
9. Watching feel good films/ comedies
10. Singing
11. Listening to music/playing an instrument
12. Socialising – in person/via social media/internet
13. Joining a choir
14. Learning something new
15. Volunteering
16. Joining a support group –in person, internet
17. Baking/cooking
18. Soup making
19. Gardening/caring for house plants/growing herbs
20. Photography
21. Drawing/painting/colouring/doodling

22. Wildlife/bird watching
23. Family tree – tracing your family history
24. DIY
25. Pottering in your shed/greenhouse/allotment/garage
26. Photo collaging/making a scrap book
27. Getting a pet/borrowing a pet
28. Crosswords/ Soduko/Jigsaw
29. Watching quiz shows
30. Finding a new hobby
31. Taking up a new sport
32. Starting a collection; stamps, antiques, pebbles, stones, shells etc
33. Enrolling on an educational course
34. Travelling
35. Trying an alternative therapy: Reiki, Acupuncture, Reflexology, Massage, Aromatherapy
36. Treating yourself to: Facial, massage, pedicure, manicure, spa treatment, retreat
37. Repairing and restoring items/treasured pieces of furniture
38. Making model aeroplanes, railways
39. Tinkering with cars/motorbikes
40. Helping others in any way possible is always a great way to make yourself feel better

This list could go on and on. I'm sure you will be able to think of other activities too.

I wish to restore your hope that you will be fine and you can adjust and grow a new life after you've suffered a loss.

The first year

This is how long it can take for you to realise just how different your life has become and for you to re-adjust to your life without your loved one.

The first year is often the hardest.

It is the anniversaries of events, special dates, birthdays, date of death, wedding anniversaries, Christmas for example which are often the most dreaded. Sometimes, however, the anticipation of the event is often worse, than the actual day itself.

You might want to mark the occasion and organise a celebration or memorial for the date, be that privately or with others.

You might want to avoid it completely and not think about it and keep yourself busy.

As these dates are reminders of your loss, be aware that your grief may resurface, feel intense again and you can feel overwhelmed or anxious about this. It is a natural reaction.

There are no rules. Do what feels right for you on these dates. Use your coping techniques to help you. Mix and match with what works best for you. Refer back to the previous chapters in the book to help you cope.

You may have already experienced some of the 'firsts' mentioned above. For example, not receiving a birthday card from them, first time you have to deal with any household matters such as dealing with the post, completing an application form alone, renewing any insurances/changing direct debit amounts, changing a light bulb, writing 'widow' on a form, arranging the boiler servicing etc.

Next time around you will know what to expect and this makes it easier to cope with.

<u>Two years on</u>

Over time the feelings of your grief will lessen.

The memories of your loved one will make you smile, not cry, and bring you some comfort and joy, not sadness.

I sincerely hope this is how you feel...

However, if this is <u>not</u> how you feel and you feel like you're getting worse not better, then you may relate to advice on the Sue Ryder website (25) and may need to seek additional help.

Likewise, if you feel your grieving is complicated in some way or you have been affected by sudden traumatic death, death by suicide or murder then you may need to seek additional help from specialists.

Please do not suffer in silence, there is help out there, speak to your GP or health professional or see Chapter 9 for additional sources of help.

Chapter 8 -
Supporting those who are
Grieving

Throughout this book my message to all is to get to know grieving and embrace grieving as part of life. By working through the chapters, I hope you now feel more prepared for grieving.

Now, I want you to keep in mind what you've learnt so far to help and support others. This chapter will explain some of the basics.

I know first-hand how hard it is to watch someone you love suffer from grief.

You can tell from a look in their eyes, their posture, their behaviour, their words and even their actions that they're struggling. Knowing what to do to help can feel frustratingly difficult.

I am not ashamed to say I have had to ask for guidance to help a loved one with her grief. Helping your nearest and dearest is not the same as helping a client, someone you've never met before. It's a different set of principles, a different set of rules, different factors involved. Love, history between you, knowing their personality, a personal relationship, a home even.

First and foremost, I have to ensure I am well, healthy and looking after myself. You've probably heard the expression about putting your own oxygen mask on first before you can help others and this is very true. Make sure you are looking after yourself both emotionally and physically. Ensure you are role modelling good behaviour and practice what you preach.

Remember you can't grieve *for* them but you can grieve *with* them.

Be mindful of the 70 + reactions from Chapter 2 and that at any time or stage they may be experiencing these. Remind yourself what they are. Don't forget, grief is not brief, it takes as long as it takes and you cannot speed up this process. Remember the caterpillar from Chapter 5? In the early months, it can take up a lot of their day processing what's happened.

Waiting while they grieve is not easy, this is where you need to remember everything you've learnt so far in this book and apply it appropriately to them. This can be a testing time for all concerned. As the saying goes, hurt people, hurt people. You may be on the receiving end of the mood swings or the signs of anxiety and depression so you'll need to be tolerant and understanding. Apply what you've learnt from this book.

I was reminded of this quote from A.A.Milne, from a famous children's book about a bear and his friends:

'Today was a Difficult Day'.

Pooh said he didn't want to talk about his difficult day. 'That's okay', said Piglet and he came and sat beside his friend. Piglet sat quietly waiting whilst Pooh worked through his difficult thoughts, knowing that his friend Piglet was there beside him and always would be.

Perhaps you can be more like piglet?

Stay by them on the outside, ready to be there for them when they are ready to reach out to you. Let them know you'll be there for them, that you'll take care of them.

You can do this by occasionally reaching in with love, food, drink, a hug, company (sitting quietly with them) and offering time to listen whilst also respecting they need their space to grieve.

If you can't be with them in person there are other ways to show you care such as a phone call, a message, card, letter, poem, video, gift an online present, send them an inspiring quote or a book for example. Food can also be associated with love and care.

Lucy's mum will always remember the kind friend who brought her home-made soups and casseroles in the first few weeks of grieving.

Remember though, appetite can be affected when grieving so don't be offended if offers of food and drink appear to be rejected, you've made the effort, that's what counts.

Like I said, it is a fine line between space and care and one of the most common themes I hear from the bereaved is avoidance. This can take many forms and is often when too much time elapses between contacting them or when those they know try to pretend they've not seen them, when they obviously have, such as crossing over the road or taking an alternative route to their usual one. Avoiding talking about the deceased or not acknowledging their death is also very upsetting for the bereaved.

I'm sure we're all guilty of doing this at some time in our lives, not just because it's awkward but sometimes due to time pressures. Now we know more about grieving, let's all make a conscious effort not to do this to others.

To help others, here's what we can do:

Acknowledge:

- When you see them, give eye contact, smile appropriately, wave appropriately
- Ask how they are, how they're doing, how they've been
- Let them lead the conversation, they will talk if they feel able to and want to
- Be prepared for the conversation to have a mixture of tears, sadness, silences and laughter too

Talking

- Talking about grieving will make it less taboo. You know it is a difficult time. You could say; how are you doing?, how are you coping?, how are you?

- Be honest, if you don't know what to say, then say that – 'I'm sorry I don't know what to say'
- Here are other things you could say – 'I'm sorry', 'I'm thinking of you' or 'I can't imagine how you feel right now' or 'I'm here for you' or I wish I could make this better for you or I can help with… or I have some lovely memories of…
- It can be tempting to say 'I know how you feel' but as you now know, this is not true, your grief experience is unique to you and we all experience grief differently. You could say how it felt for you, 'I felt like this…, when it happened to me…'
- 'Fine' is often a catch all answer which many use when in fact they are anything but fine, very much like the acronym; Feelings Inside Not Expressed, which someone gave me. If they're struggling to say how they feel, try using a number gage, so on a scale of 1 to 10, where 1 is very low and 10 is high, what number do you feel right now? This can be an alternative way to find out how they feel
- Never say to them 'it was a blessing', this is never your right to say this phrase, only they are allowed to tell you this

Listening

- Set the scene - give them an indication of how long you can spend with them; 30 minutes or all morning for example so they know your availability.
- Let them repeat the same conversation over and over. It can be hard to keep listening to the same things but it is their way of working it through and processing their thoughts.
- Allow yourself permission to listen only –to not have or know the answers, the correct replies or the right words in response, just listen attentively.

Time

- As you know, grieving takes time and we all grieve at our own pace, time is needed to heal, there are no timescales, don't rush the process, don't hurry them along, allow them time Let them be.
- Give your time to them: sit with them, just be with them. There is no need to always be talking or doing something, just being there is enough sometimes.
- Let them know you are there for them if and when-ever they do feel ready to talk.
- Avoid clichés such as 'time is a great healer', or 'he/she was a good age', whilst you know this is true, it does not make the person feel better at that specific moment in time. Instead, you could say, 'this will take time', 'it's not easy', these phrases acknowledge you understand the grieving process.
- Remember to check in with them periodically –weeks, months after.
- Acknowledge anniversaries, birthdays, significant dates, be attentive at these times as these can be especially difficult and may trigger their grief reactions.

Support

- Be kind – tell them you care, let them know if you can help and say how.
- Know that you will need to contact them even after you have sincerely said 'if there's anything you need, just ring'. Experience shows it is very difficult for the bereaved to ask directly for help so they will not ring. Nine times out of ten, you will need to contact them. If you promise to contact them then make sure you do.
- Provide emotional support by being available to listen, either in person or via other sources, phone, email, letter.

If you are unable to provide this, be honest about this but tell them what you can do to help instead.
- Practical support may be better for them or you. Make them tea, do their shopping, drive them to appointments, etc.
- Treat them how you would want to be treated if you were the one grieving.
- Helping others, helps you.

Compassion

It is human nature to try and alleviate another one's pain and it can be hard to watch someone grieving, who you know is hurting. It is natural to want them to feel better.

If you have:

Sympathy for their loss

Empathy for how it feels for them

Concern for their wellbeing

Consideration of their thoughts, feelings and behaviours

Care in your approach

Kindness with your words and actions

Love in your heart

Then all of the above will truly help others and you.

Grieving is for all, for everyone so let's help one another with this, let's be pro grief. Let us all learn the importance of grieving and how to console ourselves and others.

For life keeps moving on, that's how it has to work, it is the cycle of life, with death and grief a part of this and it has been this way for years and years and for many more to come.

Chapter 9 - Support

As a bereavement volunteer I too can be side swiped by an unexpected emotion or an intensity I was not expecting. When this happens, I have to do more to heal. I have to invest extra time and effort to mend. I am always looking, listening, searching for additional remedies to add to my own self-help tool-kit. There are lots out there, all different, to suit each and every one of us. It's just about finding the ones that can help you for the way you feel right now. We are all unique individuals and we each need to find our own personal grief pathway to come to terms with our loss.

Sometimes we need help from an external source. Here are some such organisations which can provide this help:

Cruse Bereavement Care

Founded in 1959, this charity offers support to adults, young people and children when someone dies.

www.cruse.org.uk

0808 808 1677

Email: helpline@cruse.org.uk

Survivors of Bereavement by Suicide

This charity exists to meet the needs of people over 18, bereaved by suicide.

www.uk-sobs.org.uk

0300 111 5065

Email:email.support@uksobs.org

Victim Support

An independent charity that helps people affected by traumatic events or crime to get the support they need.

www.victimsupport.org.uk

0300 303 1984

Support online can be requested via the website/telephoning

Blue Cross for pets

This charity offers a free pet bereavement support service for grieving the loss of a pet.

www.bluecross.org.uk

0300 790 9903

Email: info@bluecross.org.uk

The NHS Website

Live well – mental health, exercise, sleep, healthy body, alcohol support

www.nhs.uk

Mind

For all aspects of better mental health.

www.mind.org.uk

0300 123 3393

Email: info@mind.org.uk

British Association for Counselling and Psychotherapy (BACP)

Use the BACP directory and find the right therapist for you.

www.bacp.co.uk

01455 883300

Email: bacp@bacp.co.uk

Alcoholics Anonymous

Provides information if you are worried about your own or someone else's drinking or drug use.

www.alcoholics-anonymous.org.uk

0800 9177 650

Email: help@aamail.org

Narcotics Anonymous

If you have a drug problem, they can help.

www.ukna.org

0300 999 1212

A Final Word

This book has been in the making since 2018, since finishing my degree with honours, in Health and Social Care and achieving a distinction for the Death, Dying and Bereavement module.

Along with my years of bereavement volunteering and my many personal experiences of grieving, I wanted to share my passion and knowledge for this subject, which affects us all at some time in our lives.

From keeping a folder of varying documents, hand-outs from my bereavement supervisors, leaflets, poems and books as well as information I have learnt over the years I have always felt I needed to scoop all of this into one place – a book.

If this book makes a difference to just one person's life and saves needless suffering then I will have achieved my goal. I hope you find this pocket sized guide book, easy to read, understand and feel that you can gift it to friends, family, colleagues and others.

Heartfelt thanks to my family for allowing me the time to fulfil this dream of writing a book. Thanks to my friends, who without your personal stories of grief, your love, support and encouragement I would not have been able to make this dream a reality.

Special thanks to my bereavement buddies, supervisors and to my yoga community for growing my knowledge, wisdom and belief.

Sincere thanks to those who I have had the pleasure of helping over the years, it has been a joy to work with you and watch you heal and grow. May I continue to help many more...

A big THANK YOU to everyone who has helped me, it means the world to me.

References

1. Heegard M, When Someone Very Special Dies, Children Can Learn To Cope With Grief, 1988, 1. Change is part of life, p4

2. https://www.ons.gov.uk/peoplepopulationandcommunity/healthandsocialcare/causesofdeath, accessed on 9.8.2020

3. NHS Every Mind Matters, https://www.nhs.uk/oneyou/every-mind-matters/?WT.tsrc=Search&WT.mc_id=Brand&gclid=EAIaIQobChMI3_K8sdj56QIVwrHtCh0scwUoEAAYASAAEgLv-_D_BwE accessed on 11.6.20

4. https://www.dyingmatters.org/overview/about-us, accessed on 24.5.2020

5 .Marchant Danielle, pause, how to press pause before life does it for you, 2017, part one, nature holds you, p46

6. Losing your partner, online booklet accompanying the BBC two programme, The Widow's Tale, Chapter 9, Helping someone who has been bereaved, p17

7. https://www.change-management-coach.com/kubler-ross.html, accessed on 12/4/2020

8. https://en.wikipedia.org/wiki/Dual_process_model_of_coping, accessed 26.9.2020

9. https://www.funeralguide.co.uk/help-resources/bereavement-support/the-grieving-process/tonkins-model-of-grief#:~:text=Tonkin's%20theory%20of%20grief%20suggests,to%20find%20moments%20of%20

enjoyment.&text=This%20is%20why%20Tonkin's%20-
model%20of%20grief%20is%20called%20growing%20
around%20grief.Accessed 26.9.2020

10. Bowlby 1979:94-6, cited in Death and Dying; A Reader, Earle et al, 2009, Chapter 21, Theories of Grief: A Critical Review, p155

11. Heal, documentary, http://www.healdocumentary.com, accessed 28.06.2020

12. Morris Sue, Overcoming Grief, 2008, Chapter 3, permission to grieve,p46

13. Staudacher Carol, Men and grief, 1991, chapter 2, pages 14-25

14. Cruse Bereavement Care, Bereavement Care in Practice, The Cruse approach to working with bereaved people, 2004, p11

15. Elliot Pat, Coping with Loss, for parents, 1997, Chapter 5, Supporting a grieving child, p77

16. Nuttall Derek, 1991, The Early Days of Grieving, Chapter: What about my health, p20

17. Matsumoto Shoukei, A Monk's Guide to a Clean House and Mind, 2018, chapter 1, understanding cleaning, p3-5

18. Williams M and Penman D, Mindfulness, a practical guide to FINDING PEACE IN A FRANTIC WORLD, 2011, Chapter one, Chasing your tail, p4

19. Klass, Silverman and Nickman, Continuing Bonds, New Understandings of Grief, 1996, https://allianceofhope.org/

the-survivor-experience/aspects-of-grief/continuing-bonds/
accessed on 1.11.20

20. Much loved.com, https://www.muchloved.
fe6QIVCLrtCh0CNA5HEAAYASAAEgIgPPD_BwE,
accessed 31.5.2020

21. https://www.mnn.com/lifestyle/responsible-living/blogs/
things-do-cremated-ashes, accessed on 31.5.2020

22. Wilson Sarah, First we make the beast beautiful, 2018,
Pain is important, p189

23. Laroche Loretta, Ten simple truths that lead to an
amazing life, Life is short –wear your party pants, 2003,
Chapter 9, But what does it all mean?, p155

24. Professor Neil Frude, cited in The Little Book of
Happiness, Miriam Akhtar, MAPP, 2019, Chapter 5, p43

25. https://www.sueryder.org/how-we-can-help/someone-
close-to-me-has-died/advice-and-support/how-long-does-
grief-last, googled, accessed on 29.5.2020

Notes